2016

Born in the Scottish Borders town of Peebles, Shirley Spear grew up in Edinburgh. She began a career in journalism in Dundee, later moving to London where she met her husband, Eddie. Together they opened a restaurant on the Isle of Skye in 1984, although they had no previous experience or training. The Three Chimneys grew to gain international acclaim and was listed in the Top 50 Restaurants in the World in 2002 and 2003. Although no longer cooking and waiting professionally, Shirley and Eddie still own their island business. They remain acknowledged as having led the way in rejuvenating pride amongst Scottish chefs in the nation's culinary heritage.

D1534604

The *Three Chimneys* Marmalade Bible

Shirley Spear

Illustrated by Bob Dewar

BIRLINN

First published in 2016 by
Birlinn Limited
West Newington House
10 Newington Road
Edinburgh
EH9 1QS

www.birlinn.co.uk

ISBN: 978 1 78027 413 3

British Library Cataloguing-in-Publication Data
A catalogue record for this book is available
from the British Library

Designed and typeset by Mark Blackadder

Printed and bound by Bell & Bain Ltd, Glasgow

Contents

A Culinary Marriage Made in Heaven

(To have and to hold, to love and to cherish ...)

Marmalade. You either love it or loathe it – and I adore it. Sometimes I crave it!

Orangey, citrusy, sharp and bittersweet all meld into one delicious mouthful. Marmalade is an irresistible pleasure, a comfort food reminiscent of warm toast with mugs of tea on cold mornings. Marmalade is a taste of home, of family holidays in a seaside town with crumbly buttered oatcakes for breakfast; the perfect foil for a smoky grilled kipper, black pudding and tattie scones, or bacon, egg and sausage.

Marmalade. A true taste of Scotland or an Englishman's castle? Who invented this sensory experience and jammy delight for our taste buds? Is it the proud City of Dundee's earliest claim to culinary fame, or the descendent of a European infiltrator? How far back do recipes go?

This little book truly is a Bible in the sense that it is dedicated to all that is heaven-sent about this delicious ingredient in Scotland's remarkable culinary larder. It is dedicated to marmalade and its culinary clout, as an ingredient embedded in our national food heritage and traditional way of life.

Marmalade. It can be used in many more ways than simply spread upon toast. Use it to add flavour and zest to many items. Bake with it, roast with it, sauce and flavour with it. Season with it, spice up with it and sweeten savoury dishes too. Marmalade has a unique versatility that never fails to astonish and delight. Even those who loathe it may come to love it when they taste it in alternative ways.

Marmalade and Me

When Eddie and I took over The Three Chimneys Restaurant in October 1984, we did so with the intention of restoring faith in Scotland's larder, taking pride in its longstanding traditions and dedicating our working lives towards providing a true taste of Scottish cooking to the unsuspecting travellers who might come and discover us in our remote corner of north-west Skye.

As we worked our way through that first cash-strapped winter in Skye, planning to re-open for business at Easter time, 1985, I spent a few days in January making marmalade. This is a traditional household task for many Scots each year, when the bittersweet oranges from Seville in Spain are imported. It is a great winter pastime, filling the kitchen heart of many homes with steamy warmth and exotic fragrance. There is no doubt in my mind that my children will forever remember arriving home from school to the smell of marmalade wafting through the kitchen door, where inside yet another pot of molten amber was on a fast rolling boil upon the stove.

But how was I going to serve marmalade at lunch and dinner time? In those days, we did not have bedrooms, nor provide accommodation of any kind for our guests. As marmalade is traditionally a preserve of the breakfast table, when and how was I going to serve this iconic Scottish ingredient?

As I researched and experimented with dishes of all kinds, scaling-up household recipes for restaurant use, I was keen to include a 'nursery' pudding of some kind on my opening night menu. Nursery puddings – those associated with childhood and school meals – were very much in vogue in restaurants in the 1980s. Spotted dick, jam roly-poly, steamed suet puddings and others were enjoying a popular comeback in posher versions. In Scotland, the equivalent is clootie dumpling, a spiced, dried fruit pudding boiled in a cloth (the cloot) and served on high days and holidays across the nation. Once upon a time, every Scottish family would have had its own recipe handed down through the generations; and if I had one, I would probably add marmalade to it for extra fruitiness.

The previous owner of the restaurant had made clootie dumpling the star of his pudding menu. I wanted to make the new menu my own without reverting to the previous owner's ideas. I was determined to create a steamed pudding of a different kind in the hope that one day it would become as popular.

I had a recipe for a steamed pudding that used a mixture of apricot jam and marmalade. I decided to experiment using an all-marmalade version with my large stock of newly-made marmalade already lining the storeroom shelves. (I had begged, borrowed and cadged as many old jam jars and, better still, large Nescafé jars, from my new Skye neighbours and friends, all curious to know why I needed so many!)

The result was delicious and an immediate winner with the family. Yet one more box was ticked. I had decided upon my nursery pudding, and I was incorporating traditional marmalade into my new menu. I was delighted and I never looked back. The Three Chimneys Hot Marmalade Pudding was proudly chalked up on the pudding menu blackboards displayed in each of the two dining areas of the stone-walled cottage. On our first night, it became an immediate talking point for Eddie, who was so nervous about his brand-new role in life, serving a restaurant full of eager diners. It was a huge success and became a major draw for customers.

To this day, Hot Marmalade Pudding (recipe on p. 66) remains on the menu for both lunch and dinner at The Three Chimneys. It has never been removed and we never run out. Each winter, we still make enough marmalade to provide enough homemade for the pudding throughout the year ahead. Today, this is done on an almost industrial scale as we need such a large quantity.

Who Invented Marmalade?
Where in the World Did It Come from?

A thick paste named *marmelada* and originating from Portugal is thought to be the origin of our word for what we know today as marmalade. *Marmelada* was made from quinces, *marmelo* in Portuguese, a fruit similar in appearance to a yellow pear, but more round in shape. The Portuguese were influenced by the Romans, who used quince cooked in honey to create a preserve. This was sometimes paired with apples, pear or plums. The word *marmelo* first appears in Greek, referring to 'globular fruits', and in Latin the word *marmela* means a 'honey apple', so we can see where our word marmalade stems from and how it has developed. Similar words for jam and preserves are used throughout European languages, although, except in English, not necessarily only in connection with citrus fruits.

Arabic traders brought Chinese bitter oranges to the Mediterranean basin around 1,000 years ago. They were being grown on the island of Sicily by AD 1002, and by the twelfth century, Spaniards in the area around Seville were actively cultivating the bitter fruit. This is thought to have been the only type of citrus fruit grown in Europe for several centuries, although oranges brought to the Soller region of Majorca from Indo-China flourished in the climate there, protected by the Tramuntana Mountains.

Mary, Queen of Scots and Marmalade

In the wake of the world's earliest seafaring explorers in the late 1400s and early 1500s, Scotland always traded across the globe, importing a large range of goods. These influenced the development of the country's everyday diet and lifestyle and included bitter oranges, cane sugar and the Portuguese quince paste known as *marmelada*.

The name marmalade has been also associated with Mary, Queen of Scots, who reigned from 1542 to 1567. She is said to have found *marmelada*, a solid, sugary mass of quinces, packed and stored in a wooden box similar to a typical box of Turkish Delight, as a relief from seasickness experienced during a crossing from Calais to Scotland in 1561. *Marmelada* in these boxes is recorded as a Portuguese export in port records at the end of the fifteenth century. It was considered an aphrodisiac in Elizabethan times, and was popular when presented as a gift.

The folk tale that associates marmalade with the request by Mary (Marie malade) for *marmelada* to ease her seasickness seems to be based on a similarity of words rather than on a real incident. However, the medicinal qualities of bitter oranges are recorded from times gone by as an aid to digestion and as a treatment for wind and stomach ache. Potions made from powdered peel were used for medicinal purposes. Peel can be chewed to stave off hunger, while it was also recommended for eating after a meal, either candied or dipped in dark chocolate, as a sweetmeat. Perhaps

this is why we love it for breakfast, as it acts as a foil for the fattier content of the traditional main course?

Candied strips of citrus peel as an aid to digestion after a meal were also imported in Mary's time, and this is said to have led to the introduction of chopped peel to Scottish baking, in particular.

We do know there are several Scots culinary terms that came directly from the French language spoken by members of Mary, Queen of Scots' French entourage who lived in and around Edinburgh during her reign. This period of close French and Scottish relations is referred to as the Auld Alliance. The French word *marmelade*, used then to describe a preserve of quince and afterwards referring to a preserve of oranges, probably has led to our use of the word today.

Early Recipes

There are recipes for orange marmalade (of sorts) in the earliest cookery books published in the 1600s. Early British recipes appear to have used the peel of bitter oranges to flavour the firm, dark quince paste, but Mary Kettilby's 1714 cookery book described a concoction which used much more water, thus creating something more like a spreadable jelly.

In 1775, Mrs Elizabeth Cleland published *A New and Easy Method of Cookery*, chiefly for the benefit of the young ladies who attended her cookery school in Edinburgh's High Street, at her home near the Luckenbooths (market stalls) and St Giles Cathedral. Well-equipped kitchens had become a very important feature within the grander houses of Scotland and although female cooks would have been employed to run them, the mistress of the house was also required to have a good knowledge of cookery techniques, ingredients, table presentation and more general household management. Cleland's book contains a recipe for a shredded orange marmalade which most resembles recipes we know today.

When Samuel Johnson and James Boswell made their historic tour of the Western Isles of Scotland in 1773, spending almost half of their time in the Isle of Skye, Boswell kept a detailed diary recording the food he ate each day. His book is an immensely interesting account of life at that time, but as he was staying with the equivalent of the gentry on most occasions, his food seems to be varied, interesting and locally sourced. On 9 September, he records his breakfast of 'tea, bread and butter, marmalade and jelly, very good scones, or cakes of flour with butter'. The marmalade may not have been exactly as we know it now, but at least our visitors can be confident that delicious Seville orange marmalade, toast and home-baking still remain on the menu for breakfast in The House Over-By at The Three Chimneys in Skye today.

The Keillers of Dundee

Jute, Jam and Journalism were noted as Dundee's main industries towards the end of the nineteenth century, although during the industrial revolution, between 1760 and 1840, the city had already developed as a major east coast port.

The legend of Janet Keiller of Dundee dates from the 1700s. As a patriotic Scot, I am delighted at the idea it was her use of bitter oranges that gives us the strong connection with breakfast marmalade as we know it today!

The story goes that a cargo of bitter oranges from Spain were sold to her husband John at a bargain price by a ship sheltering from winter storms in Dundee. Janet found these impossible to sell in their shop as they were too bitter to eat, but being of a thrifty nature, she decided to turn them into jam. Rather than take time to pulp and reduce the fruit to a paste, she adopted the new French way of chopping it. Then, using plenty of water and sugar to create the preserve, she set the peel in the resulting jelly and marmalade was born.

Janet Keiller may well have learned how to make her original product using one of the old Scottish recipes to which I have referred earlier. The Keiller factory, making marmalade on a commercial scale for the first time ever, was opened in 1797. The dynasty grew rapidly from there and became one of the most important commercial companies to emerge from Dundee, with a brand name renowned throughout the world.

By the mid-1800s, in a single year, the Keillers had ordered as many as 1,500,000 printed jars in which to package marmalade for sale throughout the UK and beyond. The Maling Pottery near Newcastle produced the famous black-printed, creamy-white ceramic jars, which have become a collector's item. No doubt they were shipped quickly and conveniently to Dundee, further up the east coast.

Captain Scott's ship, the *Discovery*, was built in Dundee. As marmalade became a favourite staple of the British diet, it is interesting to note that a tin of marmalade was discovered buried in the ice, but completely intact, in the 1980s in Antarctica, where it had been taken on Scott's failed attempt to reach the South Pole in 1911. As a comfortable reminder of home it was sought after by Queen Victoria's granddaughters, one of whom became the Empress of Russia and the other the Queen of Greece. Both ladies had supplies of marmalade sent to them abroad. In 1953, Sir Edmund Hillary took a supply of marmalade with him on his ascent of Mount Everest.

Keiller's moved to larger manufacturing premises in London and was soon exporting all over the world. A patent for a process making marmalade with machinery was obtained in 1864. By the turn of the twentieth century, Keiller's had branched out into making several different products, including well-known confectionery items, mincemeat and Christmas puddings. Keiller's eventually amalgamated with another Scottish company, James

Robertson and Sons of Paisley in the west of Scotland. Robertsons became a more widely known brand name, particularly in the post-war years in the second half of the twentieth century. Today it remains a market leader, promoting the brand with assistance from the famous character Paddington Bear of children's literature. Recently it has refreshed the labelling, in keeping with Paddington's modern film-star image.

The descendents of the Keiller family used their inherited wealth to lead an academic life, based in the south of England. Alexander Keiller was a renowned archaeologist. The well-known television presenter Monty Don is also directly descended from Janet Keiller.

Scotland's Meg Dods

In 1828, 30 years after Janet Keiller reputedly made her first batch of Dundee marmalade, Mrs Margaret Dods published a new edition of her *The Cook and Housewife's Manual*, containing the 'most approved modern recipes'. This is the book most referenced by the writer F. Marian McNeill, who published *The Scots Kitchen* in 1929. Her iconic book gives a thorough account of cooking in Scotland throughout the ages, with definitive recipes for the national dishes and their associated traditions and folklore. The only recipe for marmalade that she includes in her book is Meg Dods' one for 'Scotch Orange Chip Marmalade'. Among

my most treasured possessions is a copy of Meg Dods'
original book and on page 427, I found the following recipe.

Meg Dods' recipe for marmalade

Original recipe taken from *The Cook and Housewife's Manual*,
by Mrs Margaret Dods, first published 1826.

Scotch Orange Chip Marmalade

Take equal weight of fine loaf sugar and Seville oranges.
Wipe and grate the oranges but not too much. (The grate
boiled up with sugar will make an excellent conserve for
rice, custard or batter puddings.) Cut the oranges the cross
way, and squeeze out the juice through a small sieve. Scrape
off the pulp from the inner skins, and pick out the seeds.
Boil the skins till perfectly tender, changing the water to take
off part of the bitter. When cool, scrape the coarse white
thready part from the skins, and trussing three or four skins
together for despatch, cut them into narrow chips. Clarify
the sugar, and put the chips, pulp, and juice to it. Add, when
boiled for ten minutes, the juice and grate of two lemons
to every dozen of oranges. Skim and boil for twenty
minutes; pot and cover when cold.

Today's Marmalade Awards

In 2005, Jane Hasell-McCosh, of Dalemain Mansion near Penrith in the Lake District, founded the World's Original Marmalade Awards, in a bid to grow and widen interest in the tradition of marmalade-making and to spread the love of marmalade around the globe. Dalemain is a Georgian mansion, home to Jane's family for over 300 years. When she became the mistress of the house, she discovered a rich archive of cookery books and marmalade recipes in this historic property. The whole house is a wonderful treasure trove in which the books are just one outstanding element.

Jane promotes the Marmalade Awards as an annual charity event, raising many thousands of pounds. Since its first year, the whole occasion has grown to embrace the wider area, creating a fun-packed weekend celebrating marmalade in March each year. The winners of the annual awards are announced during the festival, having been put through a serious process of judging with a panel of volunteer experts in February. Thousands of jars of marmalade arrive from all over the UK and many countries around the world. In 2016, 3,000 entries were received, including 160 from overseas countries such as Japan, Korea, Singapore and South Africa.

The winner in each category has much to gain from the whole process, for their own small business such as a B&B, or simply their personal achievement. The winner of the artisan category receives a life-changing business contract to supply Fortnum and Mason in London, where their product joins a whole range of marmalades, selected especially to represent the very best of great taste and high quality. The overall double-gold winner will also find their marmalade on sale in the renowned Piccadilly food hall. The 2016 overall winner included Talisker whisky from the Isle of Skye, the island's famous single malt. The Three Chimneys often has added a teaspoonful of this delicious peat-and-smoke pairing to its marmalade over the past 30 years and know this is a marriage made in heaven with the bittersweet tang of Seville oranges.

Making Marmalade

Marmalade Fruits

Marmalade can be made with any citrus fruits, but the traditional recipe uses bitter oranges grown in and around the beautiful city of Seville, the capital of Andalusia in southern Spain. These are available to buy in the UK for a short window of time in January and February. Almost the whole Spanish crop of Seville oranges is destined for the UK market each year.

The orange tree is an evergreen and some trees in Seville are reputed to be over 600 years old. Travellers write about the streets of Seville being lined with orange trees hanging with ripening, orange globes of fruit in winter. By springtime they are in full flower with white blossom which infuses the streets with an all-pervading fragrance.

Seville oranges are characteristically large and bitter. Spaniards say it is acceptable to pick the oranges from the trees in the streets of Seville, provided one eats the whole orange without leaving the shade of the tree!

No other citrus fruit creates the complexity of flavour

associated with Seville oranges for making traditional breakfast marmalade as we know and love it today in Scotland. Marmalade is distinct as a fruit preserve. It differs from jam or jellies as it contains the citrus fruit peel as opposed to whole berries or chopped fruit of other kinds.

True Seville oranges are not waxed before packaging and transporting. Unwaxed citrus fruit is always best to use when making marmalade. Choose fruit wisely and always wash it well before cooking. Sevilles are also a rich source of natural pectin, the setting agent necessary for all preserves. There is no need to add extra pectin products when using them to make marmalade.

There are many recipes for different citrus marmalades and methods for making it differ too. I have made lemon, lime and mixed lemon and lime marmalade and included extra lemons in a mixed fruit marmalade when making one with sweet oranges outwith the Seville season. Any combination of citrus fruits can be used, particularly pink or white grapefruit, blood oranges, kumquats, mandarins, clementines and tangerines. Some of the more unusual Japanese citrus fruits have been added to the list of possible ingredients in recent years, including yuzu, which have a delicious flavour. Lemons, particularly the large Sorrento lemons from Italy's Amalfi coast, make wonderful marmalade and are also available in the early part of the year. Soller oranges from Majorca have a distinctive flavour and are recommended for cooking with and making marmalade outside the Seville season.

Kumquats, Lemons Limes Clementines
Grapefruit Oranges Mandarins Yuzu

Mixed

ORANGES ARE NOT THE ONLY FRUIT

The chunks of orange peel in marmalade are characteristic of a real Dundee marmalade, the traditional recipe loved in Scotland today. However, some people dislike the chunks of peel intensely and this has discouraged nationwide enjoyment of this delicious preserve. Variations on the theme have been derived from the original, with the peel appearing in all sorts of shapes and sizes, but in my opinion, the traditional chunky marmalade, Dundee-style, is by far superior. The jelly should be clear and sparkling in the light, the neatly cut peel distributed evenly throughout the jar, suspended in the jelly which should be lightly set and spreadable. The true test of a good marmalade is the taste, along with the texture and set. The peel should have 'bite', but it should not be tough or too chewy.

A Few Essentials

When making marmalade at home, don't try to make too big a quantity at one go. Make sure you have large enough pans. A proper, wide-rimmed, thick-bottomed jam pan is not essential, but it is great if you have one. A copper pan is not essential either, but it will retain the heat and help the whole process. If you try to make too great a quantity, it will take a long time to come to the boil and will not boil rapidly enough to achieve a good set.

I always grease the base of the marmalade pan with a thin skim of unsalted butter before adding the ingredients.

This prevents the marmalade from sticking to the pan, which can happen when the mixture reaches a high temperature. Some people add a little bit of unsalted butter at the end of cooking to clear the marmalade of any residual scum. A whisked egg white can also be used for this purpose. I have never tried either, as I find that the scum is minimal on marmalade and soon settles when the heat is turned off and the mixture comes off the boil.

Always warm the sugar before adding it to the marmalade mixture. Do so by pouring it into a large roasting tin, or similar, and placing this in a low oven (150°C/300°F/gas 2) for at least 30 minutes, while you are preparing the rest of the recipe.

It is important to remove as much of the white pith as possible from the marmalade peel before chopping it and adding it to the marmalade mixture. Although the pith is essential for its pectin, it makes the marmalade cloudy if included at the final stage of production.

I always recommend hand-cutting the peel when making marmalade. If a blender or food processor is used, the finished product will look 'minced' in appearance and make the finished marmalade cloudy. However, I understand that some people prefer a finer cut of peel and a machine will always do the chopping more quickly. The peel of lemons and limes is best cut very finely by hand, as if shredded.

Setting Point and Wrinkle Test

Before beginning a batch of marmalade, place a few saucers or small side-plates in your freezer or the freezer compartment of a refrigerator. To test that your marmalade has reached setting point, place a teaspoonful of the hot liquid on the chilled saucer and replace it inside the freezer immediately. Leave to cool for a few minutes and then check to see if the marmalade forms wrinkles when pushed to one side with your finger tip. This is called the 'wrinkle test' and applies to all jam-making.

The setting-point temperature for jam or marmalade is higher than boiling point. This is why you must allow your marmalade to achieve and hold a fast rolling boil for up to 15 minutes, or thereabouts, to reach setting point. This is also why a large, wide-topped pan, similar in shape to a traditional jam pan, is preferable for making marmalade. The mixture will rise up the pan when boiling and needs to be held at as fast a boiling point as possible without allowing it to boil over. This part of the process demands care and attention for obvious reasons.

Potting the Marmalade

Jars and lids for potting the marmalade must be thoroughly clean and sterile. I wash these in hot soapy water first, ensuring that old labels are removed as far as possible. Rinse them well in hot running water and set aside, upturned, to drain naturally. Avoid drying with a kitchen tea towel, which can never be completely germ-free. It is not essential, but I then put the jars through a sterilising cycle in the dishwasher, allowing them to dry there too. They are then laid on the oven shelves, on a low temperature (50°C/130°F/lowest gas) to keep warm, dry and clean. Lift the jars from the oven with a clean cloth immediately before filling with marmalade, right up to the neck of the jar. Be sure to prepare your jars before starting to make the marmalade!

Always allow marmalade to settle in the pan after cooking. You will see that the peel is becoming suspended in the mixture as it cools. It should still be hot when you ladle it into the warm jars, using a soup ladle. I find a jam funnel is a very useful utensil to have when filling the jars. This is an inexpensive item and can be bought from most kitchen shops.

Jars and lids can be purchased especially for jam-making from leading kitchenware suppliers such as Lakeland. For domestic purposes, I always keep empty jars, washed and dried, ready for making marmalade and other goodies. Some of these have useful plasticised lids which can be resealed successfully when the jars are still hot. (Jars which have been in storage will require to be sterilised before using for a new batch of marmalade, as described above.)

Alternatively, traditional jam-pot covers can be purchased from kitchenware suppliers as a 'kit', suitable for typical large and small jars. The pack will contain waxed circles, cellophane covers, rubber bands and plain labels. When you have potted the marmalade, cover the surface with a waxed disc. While the jars are still hot, dampen the cellophane cover and place over the jam jar, damp side down. Secure the disc with a rubber band around the rim of the jar. The damp cellophane will shrink as it dries from the heat of the jar, forming a tight seal. Coloured paper or fabric tops can be made to cover the cellophane if liked, and these can look pretty if you are giving a jar of your homemade marmalade as a gift.

Finally, do not forget to label the jar with the name of its contents and date produced, before storing in a cool, dry cupboard.

Adding Flavours

Marmalade can be flavoured with alcohol, such as whisky, brandy or liqueurs. Many combinations have been tried and your choice is one of personal preference. As a guide, stir one teaspoonful into each average-size jar once the marmalade has been potted and allowed to cool a little. Do so with care as the jars and contents remain hot for some time. If you add alcohol to the marmalade while cooking, it will mostly evaporate.

Spices, such as cinnamon, cloves and cardamoms are popular in marmalade, and root ginger is another natural combination, particularly with lemon or lime. Spices should

be infused in the marmalade as it cooks, wrapped in a muslin bag, secured with string and hung from the handle over the side of the pan.

Stem ginger in syrup is a delicious addition. Rinse the syrup from the balls of ginger and chop these into very small chunks. Add to the marmalade when the sugar has dissolved and the mixture is beginning to come to the boil. Allow 100g (4oz) per 1kg (2lb 4oz) of fruit for good flavour, or less if you prefer.

Some people like adding fresh chopped chilli to marmalade and this is another natural combination of flavours, but perhaps eaten more happily with savoury dishes, ham or cheese, than spread on toast for breakfast.

I always add lemons in my marmalade recipe and include the peel with the orange peel in the finished mixture for extra zing. Here is the recipe that I swear by.

The Three Chimneys Traditional Seville Orange Marmalade

(This is a suitable quantity to make at home. It will make between 8 and 12 jars, depending upon the size.)

1kg (2lb 4oz) of Seville oranges
2 lemons
2l (3½pt) water
2kg (4lb 8oz) granulated sugar

Place the whole fruit in a basin of lukewarm water and give them a wash and a gentle scrub. Remove the button where the stem would have been. Place the fruit, whole, into a saucepan with the water and cover with a lid. Bring to the boil and simmer gently on a low heat for 1½–2 hours. You should be able to easily pierce the skins of the fruit when they are ready. Remove from the water and leave to cool. Reserve the water. Using a sharp knife, quarter the fruit and scrape out all the pulp and pips, right down to the peel. Too much pith left on the peel makes cloudy marmalade. Add the pips, pulp and any residual juice, into the pan with the reserved fruit water. Boil for 10 minutes and then strain through a sieve. Keep the juice and discard everything else. Pour the sugar into a flat roasting dish and put it in the oven at 150°C/300°F/gas 2 to warm through for up to an hour, while you prepare the fruit. This will make it easier to dissolve the sugar. Using a sharp knife, chop the orange and lemon peel by hand to your favourite shape. Machine cut peel makes cloudy marmalade. Butter the base of your pan with a thin skim of unsalted butter. Measure the strained juice and add extra water to make up the quantity to 1.5l (2¾pt) if necessary, as some of the original quantity will have evaporated. Put the strained juice into the pan with the chopped peel. Slowly bring to the boil. Reduce the heat, add the warm sugar and stir over a gentle heat until the sugar is completely dissolved. Put up to 12 thoroughly clean jam jars into the pre-heated oven to warm through ready for the finished marmalade. Once the sugar has dissolved, bring the mixture to the boil and continue to maintain a 'good rolling boil', without stirring, for at least 15 minutes, perhaps more. You need to reach setting point. To test for setting point: put a spoonful of marmalade on a very cold saucer previously placed in your freezer. Allow it to cool a little, and then push it with your finger, or tilt the dish to one side. If the marmalade wrinkles up, it is ready. Leave the marmalade in the hot pan until it shows that it is beginning to set. The peel will be showing signs of becoming 'suspended' in the mixture. Carefully ladle the hot marmalade into warm jam jars. It is handy to have a jam funnel for this job. Seal the jars.

For other marmalades, using different citrus fruits, follow my basic recipe above, or the alternative method described below.

Seville Orange Marmalade –
An Alternative Method

1kg (2lb 4oz) Seville oranges
1 large lemon
2.5l (4¼pt) water
2kg (4lb 8oz) granulated sugar

Wash the oranges and lemon, cut them in half, squeeze
the juice from each and put it in the marmalade pan
together with the water. Keep all the pips and any pith
which accumulate in the squeezer. Place these in a square
of muslin, laid over a saucer. Cut the orange peel into
quarters and slice according to the size you prefer in your
marmalade. Add the chopped peel to the water in the
pan. Add any more pips and pith to the muslin square.
Gather the corners of the muslin together to form a bag
and tie with string, long enough to hang from the handle
of the pan so that it is suspended in the marmalade
mixture. The pips and pith contain the pectin necessary
to make the marmalade set. Bring the mixture to
simmering point and simmer for up to 2 hours until the
orange peel is soft. Remove the muslin bag and leave it
to cool on the saucer. While the mixture is simmering,
place the sugar in a roasting tin in a very low oven to
warm. Pour the warmed sugar into the pan and stir
carefully on a low heat until it is completely dissolved.

Squeeze the bag to extract all the pectin which will ooze from the pips through the muslin. Squeeze this hard between the back of two saucers if necessary. Mix the pectin into the marmalade. Next, bring the mixture to a fast boiling point and allow this rolling boil to continue for 15–20 minutes. Test for the setting point using the wrinkle test method. Turn off the heat and allow the marmalade to settle and cool a little before potting and sealing.

Recipes

I love using marmalade in cooking . . . My own homemade is always the best – even although I may be biased! I love the chunky peel and the way the sharp, bittersweet taste of citrus fruit marries very well with all sorts of ingredients, both savoury and sweet. Commercial marmalades can be very good too (I am quite open about saying that one of these is the next best thing to my own!) and they are for sale widely. However, if you prefer a less chunky marmalade on your toast, don't be tempted to buy marmalade that has very fine peel in it for cooking, as it is less likely to be as flavoursome and is probably over-sweet. Instead, sieve the chunkier marmalade before adding it to your cooking. When buying commercial marmalade, check the sugar content and avoid those which include gelling agent or similar additives, as these are completely unnecessary. Seville oranges have a high pectin content quite naturally, so adding pectin to a commercial product is not necessary.

. . . *and Seville oranges* . . . Seville oranges can be frozen, but they are bulky, so I find it useful to zest and juice them and keep the zest and juice frozen instead. Mixed together in a small freezer container, or packed flat in freezer bags, they can be very useful to have on hand and are easy to add to a dish in preparation. Trying to grate the rind from a defrosted whole orange is not the most productive or easy kitchen task. In any case, it is always better to use ingredients when they are fresh and in season, so it is not best practice to use Seville orange zest and juice at all times of the year. There are other citrus fruits to enjoy in cooking, especially blood oranges, pink grapefruit, lemons and limes. Citrus fruits from the Far East have become a great hit in restaurant kitchens in recent times and countries in that part of the world make delicious preserves using their own native varieties.

. . . with fish, meat and game . . . In my days as Head Chef at The Three Chimneys I often used the zest and juice of Seville oranges. Seafood and bitter oranges are a natural combination. Try substituting lemons with Sevilles in hollandaise sauce with fish, for example, or in homemade mayonnaise for prawns, or in a vinaigrette dressing. They make a wonderful addition to butter for poaching and grilling, especially with lobster. Wild mallard duck, one of my all-time favourite ingredients, marries extremely well with traditional marmalade, as does anything connected with ham, bacon, chicken and cheese. It is lovely with all game, especially venison, as the herbs and spices, such as juniper, cinnamon and cloves, used for cooking game, are also a natural match with marmalade in savoury things. Port wine, Madeira, dry sherry and whisky also combine well

with marmalade in sweet or savoury dishes. Nuts, such as almonds, walnuts and hazelnuts also make a perfect pairing with marmalade, especially in baking, but also in savoury dishes.

. . . *in chutneys and preserves* . . . Adding Seville orange to homemade chutneys, such as apple, plum, apricot, date and fig, is also a winning combination. Ginger and chillies are another natural match for this wonderful fruit, and it is frequently included in spiced accompaniments. Tomato chutney would also gain from the addition of that special Seville orange taste, as do rhubarb dishes, sweet or spicy.

. . . as a glaze or refined in some way . . . Marmalade in its chunkiest form is not suitable for every recipe, as sometimes it is better to incorporate the peel in a more refined way, especially when this is required for a recipe such as Caledonian Cream, or for flavouring ice cream. Use marmalade instead of apricot jam (more usually recommended) as a glaze for a large fruit cake, prior to covering with marzipan, or as a glaze for a fruit tart, or a bakery item such as Chelsea buns. When using in any of these ways, first warm your homemade marmalade gently, liquidise it if you wish and then press it through a fine sieve to purée the peel. I always use a plastic sieve when puréeing fruit as it seems to give a better result. Press the fruit through the mesh with the base of a ladle or the back of a wooden spoon. Don't forget to scrape the residual fruit from the bottom of the sieve as it is too good to waste!

The recipes in this wee book are by no means an exhaustive list of all that can be found. I have tried to give an overall picture of just how versatile Seville orange marmalade can be in cooking. If you prefer homemade lemon or lime marmalades, these can be substituted in almost any of these recipes. But, to my mind, the original Dundee-style Seville orange marmalade, especially when homemade, is incomparable.

Cakes and Bakes

Marmalade Breakfast Scones

Makes 8 scones

250g (9oz) self-raising flour
1 rounded tsp baking powder
50g (2oz) salted butter just coming to room temperature, but not too
    soft
120ml (4fl oz) buttermilk
100g (4oz) Seville orange marmalade
Milk for glazing

Pre-heat the oven to 220°C/425°F/gas 7. Prepare a
greased baking sheet. Sieve the flour and baking powder
together into a mixing bowl. Add the butter, cut into
small chunks, and rub together until the mixture
resembles fine breadcrumbs, allowing the flour to lift and
fall into the bowl. Whisk together the buttermilk and
marmalade in another bowl. Gradually add this to the
flour mixture and work together well with the rounded-
edge blade of a table knife. The dough should be coming
together, soft and pliable, but not too wet. Lightly flour a
surface for rolling out the dough. Gently knead the
dough until it forms a smooth ball, but do not overdo
this. Handle the dough lightly and as little as possible.
Roll into a round, approximately 3cm thick. Using a
plain 6cm cutter, cut the scone shapes by pressing once,
straight down through the dough. Do not twist the
cutter. Lift and place the scone on a greased baking sheet.

Repeat until all the scones are cut, reshaping the dough and re-rolling gently until all is used. With the extra milk, lightly brush the tops of the scones. Do not allow the milk to drip over the sides if possible. Place in the centre of a hot oven for 10 minutes, until well-risen and golden brown. Remove from the oven and place the scones on a wire tray to cool. Dust with sieved flour. Serve as soon after baking as possible with fresh butter.

Marmalade Muffins

Makes 6–8 muffins
150g (5oz) plain flour
1 level tsp baking powder
1 rounded tsp ground cinnamon
Juice of 1 orange (approx. 120ml, 4fl oz)
2 heaped tbsp chopped hazelnuts
1 large egg
50g (2oz) butter, melted and cooled slightly
2 tbsp chunky dark marmalade

To finish
1 tbsp melted marmalade
1 tbsp chopped hazelnuts

Get all the ingredients ready before you start, prepare the
muffin tin and pre-heat the oven at 200°C/400°F/gas 6.
Measure the squeezed orange juice into a jug. You
require 120ml (4fl oz). Add milk if more liquid is needed
to make this quantity. Tip the marmalade into a bowl and
loosen it up with the back of a wooden spoon, which
will make it easier to fold it into the muffin mixture.
Sieve the flour, baking powder and cinnamon into a
bowl, lifting the sieve high to incorporate as much air as
possible. In another bowl, whisk the egg, orange juice,
milk and melted butter together, and add the hazelnuts.
Sieve the dry ingredients for a second time into the egg

and butter mixture. Fold the ingredients together quickly, using a large metal spoon. Fold in the marmalade, again quickly, to avoid over-mixing which will make the muffins dense in texture. Divide the mixture between the muffin cases. Bake in the centre of the oven for 25 minutes until well-risen and golden. Remove from the oven and place on a wire rack to cool immediately. Brush with the extra marmalade and sprinkle the extra hazelnuts on top. These will store in an airtight tin, but are best served fresh and warm for breakfast.

Marmalade Flapjacks

200g (7oz) butter, slightly salted
150g (5oz) soft light brown sugar
2 tbsp chunky Seville orange marmalade
2 tbsp golden syrup
300g (10oz) porridge oats
75g (3oz) dried apricots, chopped small
75g (3oz) chopped dates
50g (2oz) desiccated coconut

Butter a 28cm x 18cm baking tin. Pre-heat the oven to
150°C/300°F/gas 2. Melt the butter, sugar, marmalade
and golden syrup in a saucepan and stir together. In a
baking bowl, mix together the porridge oats, dried fruit
and coconut. Pour the melted ingredients over the dry
ingredients and mix together well. Transfer the mixture
to the baking tray and spread evenly, corner to corner.
Level the surface with a palette knife. Place in the centre
of the oven and bake for 50 minutes or until golden
brown. Remove from the oven and lightly score into bars
while still warm. Leave to cool completely before cutting
and removing from the tin. Melted chocolate could be
drizzled on top of the cooled flapjacks, if liked. Store in
an airtight tin once the chocolate has set.

Whisky Fruit Loaf

This has been a popular cake to serve with a welcoming cuppa to our guests arriving to stay with us at The Three Chimneys and The House Over-By. Sometimes we put a thick slice into a picnic lunch too.

175g (6oz) raisins
175g (6oz) sultanas
150g (5oz) currants
225ml (8fl oz) water
110g (4oz) butter
150g (5oz) soft dark brown sugar
3 eggs, beaten
275g (10oz) self-raising flour
2 tsp mixed ground spice
2 heaped tbsp Seville orange marmalade
25g (1oz) nibbed almonds
110g (4oz) chopped glacé cherries
110g (4oz) chopped mixed peel
4 tbsp whisky

Grease two 2lb (1kg) loaf tins with a little butter and line with parchment paper. Pre-heat the oven to 180°C/350°F/gas 4. Put the raisins, sultanas, currants, water, butter and brown sugar into a large saucepan. Heat slowly until the butter has melted completely. Take the pan off the heat and allow to cool down for a few minutes. Add the beaten eggs, sieved flour, spice, marmalade, cherries, peel, almonds and whisky. Mix

thoroughly. Pour the mixture into the prepared loaf tins. Put on the centre shelf of the pre-heated oven and bake for 1 hour. The finished cake should be a deep golden brown. Cool in the loaf tins for at least 30 minutes before turning on to a wire tray to cool completely. Store in an airtight tin until ready to use. This fruit loaf also freezes very well.

Marmalade Tea Cake

This makes a wonderful tea loaf which can be stored for a good length of time in an airtight tin, or frozen for another occasion. Don't forget to put the fruit to soak overnight.

_____

110g (4oz) raisins
110g (4oz) currants
110g (4oz) sultanas
75g (3oz) Seville orange marmalade
25g (1oz) Demerara sugar
150ml (5fl oz) strong hot tea made with a tea bag in a cup
    (ordinary breakfast tea is good)
50g (2oz) chopped roasted hazelnuts
1 large egg
225g (8oz) self-raising flour
1–2 tbsp milk

_____

Start the night before . . .
Place the dried fruit, marmalade and Demerara sugar into a bowl and mix together. Make the tea and pour it over the fruit. Leave covered overnight, to allow time for the fruit to soak up the tea.

The next day . . .
Pre-heat the oven to 180°C/350°F/gas 4. Line a standard 2lb (1kg) loaf tin with non-stick parchment paper. Whisk the egg and add it to the fruit mixture. Sift in the flour.

Add the chopped nuts. Mix together well. You are aiming to achieve a good dropping consistency and may require some of the milk, but do not add all of it at once. Add *some* or *all* of the milk as required. Spoon the mixture into the prepared loaf tin and level it off with the back of a spoon dipped in cold water. Place on a low shelf in the oven and bake for up to 1 hour 10 minutes, until it feels springy to touch in the centre. Remove from the oven and leave in the tin on a cooling rack until cold. Serve cut in thick slices, spread with butter. This loaf keeps well in an airtight tin and is also delicious toasted.

The night before

Marmalade Date and Walnut Loaf Cake

225g (8oz) plain flour
3 level tsp baking powder
110g (4oz) soft dark brown sugar
110g (4oz) soft butter
Zest of 1 large orange
1 level tsp mixed spice
50g (2oz) chopped walnuts
50g (2oz) chopped dates
2 heaped tbsp Seville orange marmalade
150ml (5fl oz) milk

For the topping:
1 tbsp Demerara sugar

Line a standard 2lb (1kg) loaf tin with non-stick parchment paper. Pre-heat the oven to 180°C/350°F/gas 4. Combine the sieved flour, baking powder, mixed spice and soft dark brown sugar in a mixing bowl. Add the butter to the dry ingredients and rub in with finger tips until the mixture resembles fine breadcrumbs. Add the orange zest, chopped walnuts and dates. Mix again lightly, lifting the mixture high to encourage air into the mixture. Add the marmalade and mix everything together well. Add the milk in stages until a good dropping consistency is achieved. You may not need all of

LIFT THE MIXTURE HIGH

it or you might need a little more. Spoon the mixture into the prepared baking tin and level the surface with the back of a spoon. Sprinkle the Demerara sugar over the top. Bake on the lower shelf of the oven for 1 hour until the cake feels firm in the centre. It may need a little longer than 1 hour, but after 50 minutes, place a piece of foil or baking parchment loosely over the surface, to prevent the Demerara sugar from burning on the surface of the cake. When baked, remove from the oven and leave the cake to cool in the tin, set aside on a cooling rack. When cold, serve sliced with, or without, butter. This cake keeps well in an airtight tin.

Sticky Marmalade Ginger Cake

175g (6oz) butter
150g (5oz) soft light brown sugar
2 eggs
25g (1oz) black treacle
125g (4½oz) marmalade
25g (1oz) crystallised ginger pieces
Zest of 1 orange
Juice of ½ orange
175g (6oz) self-raising wholemeal flour

Pre-heat the oven to 180°C/350°F/gas 4. Prepare a loaf
tin measuring 22cm x 12cm x 6cm lined with non-stick
parchment paper. Cream the butter and sugar together.
Beat the eggs and treacle together and add little by little
to the butter and sugar. Add the marmalade, ginger
pieces, orange zest and orange juice and beat together
well. Fold in the flour. Spoon the mixture into a deep
loaf tin. Place in the centre of the oven and bake for 35
minutes, until risen and firm to touch. Remove from the
oven, glaze with a spoonful of warm marmalade and
leave to cool completely. Serve sliced.

Lemon Marmalade Cake

This recipe uses lemon marmalade, but other flavours of marmalade can be used too.

175g (6oz) unsalted butter
175g (6oz) golden caster sugar
3 eggs, beaten
150g (5oz) self-raising flour
25g (1oz) ground almonds
½ tsp baking powder
3 tbsp lemon marmalade
1 lemon, zest and juice

For the topping:
2 tbsp lemon marmalade
100g (3½oz) icing sugar

Line a 20cm round, loose-bottomed deep cake tin with non-stick parchment paper. Pre-heat the oven at 180°C/350°F/gas 4. Cream the butter and sugar together until light and fluffy. Beat in the eggs a little at a time. Fold in the sieved flour and baking powder. Stir in the marmalade, plus the lemon zest and juice. Pour the mixture into the prepared tin and bake in the centre of the oven for 45–50 minutes until golden brown and springy to touch in the centre. Remove from the oven and leave in the tin, standing on a cooling rack. Melt the lemon marmalade in a small saucepan and brush all over the surface of the cake while it is still warm. Leave to cool completely. When cold, remove from the tin and stand the cake on the cooling tray, with a baking sheet underneath it. Mix the sieved icing sugar with 2 tbsp warm water and stir well to make a smooth icing. Pour this over the glazed cake, allowing the icing to drip down the sides of the cake. Any residual icing will collect on a tray placed underneath the cooling rack. Leave to set before serving, cut into wedges for afternoon tea.

Carrot and Marmalade Cake with Marmalade Frosting

150 ml (5fl oz) Scottish rapeseed oil
2 eggs
140g (5oz) soft light brown sugar
85g (3oz) wholemeal self-raising flour
85g (3oz) white self-raising flour
2 tsp each ground cinnamon and mixed spice
1 tsp bicarbonate of soda
50g (2oz) sultanas
1 tbsp Seville orange marmalade
150g (5oz) carrot grated
50g (2oz) chopped walnuts, plus a few half walnuts for garnish

Whisk the eggs with the oil and set aside. In a bowl, mix together the sugar, flour, spices and bicarbonate of soda, then add the sultanas, marmalade, carrots and chopped walnuts. Mix together well. Add the egg and oil mixture. Put the mixture into the prepared loaf tin and place in the centre of the oven. Bake for 1 hour until risen, golden and springy to touch, remove and set aside to cool in the tin completely.

For the frosting
200g (7oz) soft cream cheese, or crowdie cheese mixed
    with 1 tbsp cream
50g (2oz) soft Scottish butter
50g (2oz) sieved icing sugar
1 tbsp Seville orange marmalade
Pinch of ground cinnamon

To finish:

Beat together the soft cheese and the soft butter, and add
the marmalade, icing sugar and ground cinnamon. Mix
together really well to form a creamy frosting. Remove
the cake from the tin, spread the surface with the frosting
and decorate with walnut halves. Slice and serve!

Dundee Marmalade Fruit Cake

175g (6oz) currants
175g (6oz) sultanas
50g (2oz) chopped mixed peel
50g (2oz) glacé cherries, quartered
1 generous tbsp Seville orange marmalade
225g (8oz) self-raising flour
¼ tsp ground mixed spice
175g (6oz) Scottish butter, slightly salted
175g (6oz) soft light brown sugar
3 eggs
1 tbsp milk
Whole blanched almonds for decoration

Pre-heat the oven 180°C/350°F/gas 4. Prepare a deep,
20cm cake tin, lining the base and sides with non-stick
parchment paper.

Cream together the butter and sugar. Add the beaten
eggs, one at a time. Fold in the sieved flour and spice.
Add the dried fruit, peel, cherries and marmalade. Mix
well. If the mixture seems a little stiff, add the milk. You
are aiming for a good dropping consistency. Put all the
mixture into the prepared tin and level the surface.
Decorate the surface with a symmetrical pattern of
almonds pressed lightly on top. Bake in the oven at
180°C/350°F/gas 4 for 1 hour. Turn down the oven to
very low, 140°C/275°F/gas 1, for another hour. The cake

should be risen and golden brown. Test with a skewer to ensure the cake is cooked right through. The skewer should be inserted into the middle of the cake, and when removed it should come out clean. Remove from the oven and leave to cool completely in the tin on a cooling rack. The cake will keep well in an airtight tin, wrapped in clean greaseproof paper.

Marmalade Cheesecake

Please note this recipe uses raw eggs which you may wish to avoid eating.

This cheesecake can be made with your favourite flavour of marmalade and is very good with lemon, lemon and lime, or lime and ginger marmalade, which also marries well with summer strawberries, raspberries, frosted grapes or passion fruit juice.

Serves up to 12

For the base
1 x 225g (8oz) packet of digestive biscuits
110g (4oz) butter, melted

Lightly oil a deep, 23cm loose-bottomed cake tin. Crush the biscuits in a food processor, or place them in a polythene bag and crush with a rolling pin. Place the biscuit crumbs into a mixing bowl. Pour the warm melted butter over the crumbs. Stir well. Cover the base of the cake tin with the buttered crumbs in an even layer and pat down with the base of a potato masher, a flat spatula or palette knife. Set aside in the refrigerator.

For the cheese topping

2 x 140g tubs (9oz) Scottish crowdie cheese
150ml (5fl oz) fresh double cream
50g (2 oz) golden caster sugar
Juice of 1 lemon
2 large eggs, separated
2 generous tbsp Seville orange marmalade
2 tsp powdered gelatine, dissolved in 2 tbsp warm water

Place the crowdie cheese, cream, sugar, lemon juice and egg yolks into a bowl or food processor and mix well until very smooth. Put the gelatine powder into a small, non-stick saucepan and pour the warm water over it. Stir well on a very low heat and add the marmalade, stirring all the time. When all is completely combined, add this to the cheese mixture and mix together well. Whisk the egg whites in a clean, grease-free bowl until they form soft peaks. Carefully fold the whites into the cheese mixture, combining well. Pour the finished mixture into the baking tin to cover the biscuit base. Place in the refrigerator to set. Just before serving, remove from the refrigerator and remove the cheesecake from the tin by pushing from the bottom upwards. Decorate with fresh fruit of your choice. Strawberries are a lovely combination with the orange flavours.

Puddings and Pies

PUDDINGS
AND PIES

POT
TATE
O

The Three Chimneys
Hot Marmalade Pudding

Serves up to 8

150g (6oz) fine brown breadcrumbs
110g (4oz) soft light-brown sugar
25g (1oz) self-raising wholemeal or white flour
110g (4oz) butter, plus extra for greasing the bowl
8 tbsp well-flavoured, coarse-cut Seville orange marmalade
3 large eggs
1 rounded tsp bicarbonate of soda, plus 1 tbsp water

Butter a two-litre/three-pint pudding basin, preferably a
plastic one with a clip-on lid. Place the breadcrumbs,
flour and sugar in a mixing bowl. Gently melt the butter
with the marmalade. Pour the melted ingredients over
the dry ingredients and mix thoroughly. Whisk the eggs
until frothy and gently beat into the mixture until
combined. Dissolve the bicarbonate of soda in the water,
then stir into the mixture, which will increase in volume
as it absorbs the bicarbonate of soda. Spoon the mixture
into the pudding basin immediately. Cover with a close-
fitting lid *or* make a lid with circles of buttered greaseproof paper and foil, pleated together across the centre
and tied securely around the rim of the basin. Place the
basin in a saucepan of boiling water. The water should
reach halfway up the side of the basin. Cover the pan

with a lid and simmer for two hours. The water will need topping up throughout this period. Turn out onto a dish, slice and serve hot, with cream, ice cream, thick natural yoghurt, or crème fraîche, or – as we like to do at The Three Chimneys – with Drambuie Custard.

Caledonian Cream

This is delicious served on its own or with fruit of any
kind, including poached apples, plums, apricots and pears,
plus all the soft fruits of summer. At The Three Chimneys
we have used it to sandwich together homemade
meringues, served with fresh strawberries.

_____

2 heaped tbsp Seville orange marmalade warmed gently and then
    sieved through a plastic mesh with the back of a wooden
    spoon to 'mince' the peel
1 x 140g (4.5oz) tub of traditional Highland crowdie cheese
200ml (7fl oz) fresh double cream
2–3 generous tbsp blended Scotch whisky
2 tbsp lemon juice

_____

Sieve the warmed marmalade into a mixing bowl. Add
the lemon juice and whisky and mix well, then add the
crowdie cheese and the double cream. Beat together
with a whisk until the cheese is much smoother and
combines well with the other ingredients. Add more
whisky or lemon juice if necessary to suit your own taste.
Spoon into a serving dish and refrigerate until ready to
use. Toasted medium oatmeal can be sprinkled on top if
liked.

Old-Fashioned Fruity Bread Pudding

Serves up to 12

450g (1lb) left-over stale bread
575ml (1pt) fresh milk
100g (3½oz) chopped candied peel
Zest of 1 orange and 1 lemon
200g (7oz) currants
100g (3½oz) sultanas
100g (3½oz) raisins
50g (2oz) chopped dates
75g (3oz) demerara sugar
4 heaped tsp ground mixed spice
2 large tbsp homemade chunky marmalade
150g (5oz) chilled Scottish salted butter
2 large eggs, whisked
Whole nutmeg for grating on top
Caster sugar for serving

Butter a three-pint/two-litre pie dish, or similar baking dish, such as a typical lasagne dish. Pre-heat the oven to 180°C/350°F/gas 4. Break the bread into small pieces and place in a large baking bowl. Pour over the milk and leave to soak for up to 30 minutes, covered with a cloth. Add all the other ingredients except the eggs. Mix together well. Grate the butter on the large side of the grater into the mixture. Add the whisked eggs and stir everything together well. Use a cutting action with a large metal spoon to distribute the butter through the

mixture. The finished mixture should be of a dropping consistency. Spoon the mixture into the dish and distribute evenly. Drag the back of a fork across the pudding. Grate fresh nutmeg all over the top generously. Place on the low shelf of a pre-heated oven. Bake for up to 2 hours in total, until brown and firm to the touch. Serve while hot, or leave to cool completely and reheat individual portions. Sprinkle with caster sugar before serving with fresh double cream, pouring cream, custard or ice cream.

Dark Chocolate Marmalade Tart

Serves up to 12

Prepare the pastry case:
Pre-heat a flat baking sheet in the centre of a moderate oven, 180°C/350°F/gas 4. Line a fluted flan tin with pastry and prick the base all over. Cover the pastry case with a circle of non-stick baking paper and cover with a layer of baking beans, or a dry ingredient such as uncooked rice or lentils. Place in the oven and bake for 15 minutes. Remove the flan case from the oven and carefully remove the paper and baking beans. Brush the whole base and sides of the pastry case with whisked egg. Return to the oven for a further 10 minutes until starting to turn golden brown and crisp. Remove from the oven and set aside for filling. Turn down the temperature of the oven to 140°C/275°F/gas 1.

While the tart case is baking, prepare the filling as follows.

225g (8oz) dark chocolate
150g (5oz) unsalted butter
3 whole eggs
2 whole yolks
50g (2oz) caster sugar
1 generous tbsp Seville orange marmalade

Melt together the chocolate and butter slowly in a bowl over a pan of simmering hot water. Do not allow the bowl to touch the water. Stir occasionally to ensure all is mixed together well.

In another bowl, whisk together the whole eggs, egg yolks, sugar and marmalade. Mix half of the chocolate mixture into the egg and marmalade mixture. Fold the other half into the mixture gently. Pour the whole lot into the pre-cooked pastry case. Return to the oven and bake slowly for 25-30 minutes until risen. Once removed from the oven, the chocolate filling will have a little bit of 'wobble' and will set when it cools, when it can be cut and served with fresh double cream or ice cream.

Chocolate Marmalade Mousse Cake

225g (8oz) unsalted butter
225g (8oz) dark chocolate
50g (2oz) ground almonds
150g (5oz) plain white flour
6 eggs, separated
2 generous tbsp Seville orange marmalade
75g (3oz) caster sugar
Icing sugar to dust finished cake

Pre-heat the oven to 180°C/350°F/gas 4. Prepare a deep, 23cm loose-based cake tin, lining the base and sides with non-stick baking parchment.

Melt the chocolate and butter together in a bowl over a pan of simmering hot water. Do not allow the base of the bowl to touch the water. Keep on a medium heat and stir from time to time. Whisk the egg yolks and marmalade until they are thick and creamy. Fold in the sieved flour and ground almonds. Add the melted chocolate and butter and mix thoroughly. Whisk the egg white and caster sugar to soft peak stage and fold into the chocolate mixture. Pour into the prepared tin. Place in the pre-heated oven and bake for 40-45 minutes. The cake should feel just 'set' to touch. Remove from the oven and set aside to cool. The cake may sink, but that's OK! Remove from tin, dust with sieved icing sugar and serve with fresh cream or crème fraîche.

Vegetables and Accompaniments

Glazed Marmalade Carrots

Delicious with poultry, gammon or game, especially roast quail, partridge, pheasant or wild duck.

Makes 4 portions
1kg (2lb 4oz) carrots, cleaned and cut into batons
250ml (8fl oz) water
50g (2oz) marmalade
25g (1oz) butter
25g (1oz) golden caster sugar
Chopped parsley to garnish

Place the water in a saucepan together with all the ingredients except the carrots and parsley. Warm gently until the butter, sugar and marmalade are beginning to dissolve. Add the carrots, bring to the boil and simmer gently for 20 minutes without a lid, until the liquid has evaporated and the carrots are left coated in the glaze. Sprinkle with parsley before serving hot.

Roasted Beetroots with Marmalade

You can be baking or cooking other items in the oven while the beets cook gently on a low shelf. They will come to no harm if the oven is at a lower temperature, but take a bit longer to tenderise. Plan whatever is most convenient. Once cooked, the beets will keep refrigerated in a container for 1 week and can be used hot or cold.

500g (1lb 2oz) raw beets, a mixture of colours if possible
A bunch of fresh thyme

For the glaze
2 tbsp Seville orange marmalade
50g (2oz) butter
2 heaped tsp horseradish sauce
Salt and pepper

Wash the beets, remove the stems and leaves. Place the whole beetroot in a roasting tin, lined with foil. Add enough water to cover the base of the tin to a depth of 5mm. Scatter sprigs of thyme on top. Cover with a sheet of foil and bake on a low shelf in a pre-heated oven, 190°C/375°F/gas 5, for at least 1 hour until the beets are tender. Remove from the oven, discard the sprigs of thyme and leave the beets to cool. Turn the oven temperature up to 220°C/425°F/gas 7 for glazing. Melt the ingredients for the glaze in a saucepan. Peel and cut the cooled beetroot into wedges or thick slices. Return to the roasting tin, re-lined with a clean sheet of foil. Pour the melted glaze over the beetroot and turn the beetroot in the glaze until well coated. Season with salt and pepper. Return to a high shelf in a hot oven. Cook for a further 20 minutes until glazed and sizzling hot. Serve as an accompaniment for roast ham, pork or duck.

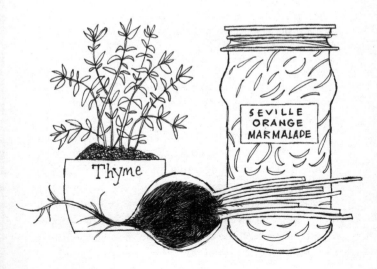

Braised Red Cabbage
with Marmalade

Delicious served with roast pork, venison or duck.

Serves up to 6

500g (1lb 2oz) red cabbage, very thinly shredded (equivalent of
    1 small/medium-size cabbage)

1 large onion, peeled and chopped small

4 large cloves garlic, crushed

1 large cooking apple, peeled, cored and chopped small

2 tbsp cider vinegar

2 tbsp Seville orange marmalade

Juice of ½ a large orange

25g (1oz) salted butter

Freshly ground black pepper and sea salt

Whole nutmeg for grating

6 juniper berries crushed

8 whole cloves

½ cinnamon stick broken roughly into pieces

Piece of root ginger about the size of a brazil nut, sliced thinly

---

Pre-heat the oven to 150°C/300°F/gas 2. Wrap the
crushed juniper berries, whole cloves, broken cinnamon
stick and sliced root ginger in a muslin square. Melt the
marmalade in a saucepan with the orange juice and cider
vinegar. Make a layer of half the finely sliced red cabbage
in a deep, ovenproof dish. Cover with a layer of chopped
onion, mixed with the crushed garlic and chopped apple.
Dot with butter. Season with salt, pepper and grated

nutmeg. Pour over half the marmalade and vinegar mixture. Bury the spices wrapped in muslin in this mixture. Cover with another layer of red cabbage. Season again with salt, pepper and nutmeg. Pour over the remaining marmalade and cider vinegar. Dot with more butter. Cover with a layer of greaseproof paper and either a close-fitting lid, or a layer of foil. Place on a low shelf of a pre-heated oven and cook slowly for up to 2 hours. Remove the muslin bag of spices and check the seasoning before serving.

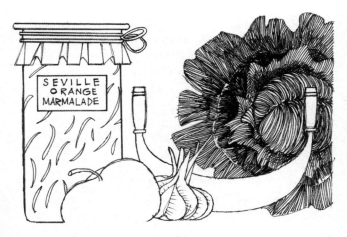

Marmalade Apple Sauce

For serving with roast or grilled pork.

Enough for 4
2 Bramley cooking apples
Juice of ½ a large orange
2 tbsp Seville orange marmalade
¼ tsp ground cinnamon
25g (1oz) unsalted butter

Peel, quarter and core the apples, then chop into small
pieces. Place the apples in a saucepan, together with the
orange juice, marmalade and cinnamon. Add half the
butter and place the pan on a low heat. Allow the apples
to warm through and become very soft and pulpy. This
does not take long. Turn off the heat, add the remaining
butter and beat the apple with a wooden spoon until
puréed. Leave in a warm place with the lid on until ready
to serve. The apple sauce should need no seasoning,
especially if you are serving it with
roast pork and salty crackling.

Rhubarb and Marmalade Sauce

This is a delicious, traditional accompaniment to grilled mackerel or herring fillets. Alternatively, coat the fresh fish fillets in medium oatmeal and fry in butter for a few minutes on each side.

Enough for 4, or up to 8 fish fillets
3 sticks of garden rhubarb, washed and cut into 3cm chunks
2 tbsp Seville orange marmalade
1 piece of root ginger (about the size of the top half of your thumb)
Juice of ½ a large orange (you will need the other half of the orange
    for garnish, plus a little extra squeeze of juice to complete
    cooking the fish)
Soft brown sugar to sweeten to taste (optional)

Place the chopped rhubarb into a small saucepan that has a close-fitting lid. Add the marmalade, finely grated root ginger and orange juice to the pan. Mix well and place on a very low heat, cover with the lid. Allow to cook gently for around 10 minutes, until the rhubarb has broken up and become pulpy. Remove from the heat and beat the cooked rhubarb with a wooden spoon for a minute until it becomes even more puréed. Push the puree through a plastic sieve into a clean bowl with the back of your wooden spoon. Keep pushing the purée through until all the rhubarb has been used. Don't forget to scrape the purée from the base of the sieve, as the thick fruit will also collect there. Warm gently before

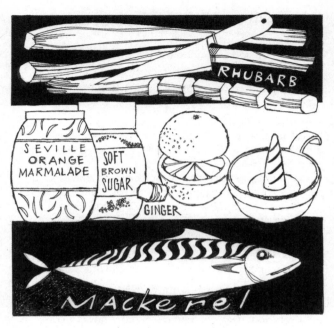

serving with the cooked mackerel or herring fillets. If required, add soft brown sugar to the rhubarb and orange purée, in small quantities, according to taste, when re-heating. Stir it well until dissolved. Do not over-sweeten, as this is recipe should be sharp to accompany the savoury fish.

Meat and Fish Dishes

Roast Gammon Joint with Mustard and Marmalade Glaze

_____

Serves between 8 and 12

1 unsmoked gammon joint ready to cook, weighing approximately
    2kg (4½lb)

1 x 330ml (12fl oz) can of strong cider

Peel of 1 orange, removed with a potato peeler (reserve juice)

I large onion, peeled and cut in half and studded with cloves

12 cloves (optional)

1 tsp black peppercorns (no salt is required)

4 fresh bay leaves

_____

To cook the gammon

Cooking time is divided between boiling and roasting.
Allow 25 minutes per ½ kg (1lb 2oz) plus 25 minutes
over, so in total, e.g. for a joint weighing 2kg (4½lb),
allow a total time of 2 hours and 5 minutes. Boil for 1
hour. Roast for 1 hour plus extra time depending on
weight. Slow-cooking benefits this cut of meat and
prevents it from becoming chewy. It will carve very well
and stretch a long way, so it is excellent for big parties or
family get-togethers.

    To boil, place the whole joint in a large saucepan,
cover with cold water. Bring to the boil and then turn
off the heat. Lift the joint out of the water and stand on a
dish. Pour away the water and rinse out the pan. Replace
the meat in the pan, add the other ingredients. Add

enough cold water to cover the meat. Return to the stove, bring to the boil, cover with a lid and simmer gently for half the total cooking time. (Pre-heat the oven at 180°C/350°F/gas 4 while waiting for the gammon to boil.) Turn off the heat under the boiling pan and carefully remove the gammon and stand on a dish as before. Carefully strain the liquid into a bowl or large jug and set aside as stock for soup. Discard the other ingredients. Place the gammon in a roasting dish, covered loosely with foil. Roast for three-quarters of the total amount of time allowed for second stage of cooking. (This allows for 20 minutes or a little more, to finalise the cooking and the glaze, at the final stage.)

To glaze the gammon

Juice of a large orange
4 large tbsp homemade chunky Seville orange marmalade
4 heaped tsp strong grainy mustard
50g (2oz) soft dark brown sugar
Cloves for decoration

Prepare the glaze while the gammon is roasting in the oven. Place all the ingredients in a saucepan and melt together. Stir well and set aside in a warm place until ready to use. Remove the gammon after the required roasting time and stand on a dish. When it is cool enough to handle, gently remove the darker, top layer of skin, leaving the second layer of pale fat intact. The skin will pull away quite easily. You may want to start it off by easing the point of a knife under one corner and then, gripping the skin with a piece of kitchen roll, pull it away from the next layer of fat. Score the fat in a diagonal diamond pattern all over the joint. Stud with cloves if liked, at regular intervals. Return the joint to the roasting tin. Little by little spoon the warm glaze all over the joint, allowing it to run into the scored fat and down the sides. Return to the oven and finish roasting until the glaze is golden and glistening. You may want to baste the gammon at intervals, spooning the glaze back over the gammon as it runs into the roasting tin. Take care as this will be hot. You can allow around 20 to 30 minutes to complete the cooking process at the final stage. Carve and serve immediately with vegetables of your choice. Excess glaze can be handed around as a sauce. Alternatively, leave to cool completely overnight and keep refrigerated until ready to use for a party or breakfast buffet, or as a useful cut-and-come-again joint for a number of days to use at mealtimes, for sandwiches, etc. Cover the cooked gammon in baking parchment paper to avoid the glaze sticking to the wrapping.

Roast Duck with Port and Marmalade Sauce

Serves up to 4

1 oven-ready duck
2 tbsp Scottish rapeseed oil
1 large onion, peeled and cut into eight pieces
1 large carrot, peeled and cut into eight chunks
1 large stick of celery from the outer bunch, washed and cut into
    chunks, plus a few leaves from the centre of the bunch
4 cloves garlic, peeled and roughly chopped
A few sprigs of fresh parsley, with stalks
A handful of fresh sage leaves
Freshly ground rock salt and black pepper
2 heaped tbsp Seville orange marmalade
Juice of 1 large orange
4 tbsp ruby port
20g (1oz) soft butter

Heat the oven to 200°C/400°F/gas 6 and prepare a roasting tin for the duck, lined with foil. Heat the rapeseed oil in a heavy frying pan and add the prepared vegetables. Cook until beginning to soften, season with salt and pepper and add the fresh herbs. Stir well and spoon the mixture into the roasting tin, covering the base. Place the duck on top of the vegetables. Put the marmalade, orange juice and port into the hot frying pan and heat through. Pour this mixture over the top of the duck and vegetables. Season the duck with a little more salt and pepper. Take a sheet of parchment or greaseproof paper and butter it on one side. Place the paper, butter-side down, on top of the duck and put on the middle shelf of a pre-heated oven for 75 minutes. Half an hour before roasting time is complete, remove the paper and baste the duck with the collected juices in the tin. Return the uncovered duck to the oven to cook for a further 10 minutes before removing from the oven again and lifting the duck on to a dish. Pour the contents of the roasting tin through a strainer into a saucepan. Replace the duck in the roasting tin and return to the oven to complete the cooking time and allow the surface to turn golden brown. Discard the cooked vegetables and herbs. Re-heat the cooking juices in a saucepan and keep warm. Once the duck is cooked, lift it on to a carving board to rest in a warm place. Pour any more cooking juices from the roasting tin into the sauce and whisk all together well, while allowing the sauce to reduce and emulsify. Taste for strength of flavour as well as seasoning and add a little hot vegetable water from a pot cooking the accompaniments, or a dash more port, or more marmalade, as required. When carving, more juices may escape, so pour these into the sauce too. Before serving, strain the sauce through a sieve into a sauceboat or similar. Serve the duck with the sauce poured over the meat, with accompanying vegetables of your choice. Roast parsnips would be excellent, perhaps with mashed sweet potato and finely shredded Savoy cabbage.

Warm Salad of Seared Scallops with Marmalade and Grainy Mustard Dressing

Serves 4 as a starter
8 medium or king-size scallops, cleaned and prepared
A selection of fresh salad leaves

For the dressing
1 tbsp Seville orange marmalade
1 tbsp sherry vinegar
1 tsp grainy mustard
Freshly ground salt and black pepper
150ml (5fl oz) good quality hazelnut oil

To make the dressing, melt the marmalade and sieve the contents into a bowl or jug. Add the vinegar and grainy mustard. Mix well and gently whisk the oil into the dressing until it begins to thicken slightly. Set aside until ready to use, when it should be warmed gently.

To cook and serve, heat one to two tablespoons of olive oil in a small thick-based frying pan. The pan should be very hot. Before searing the scallops in the hot oil, pat them dry between sheets of kitchen towel and pierce the coral roes with the point of a sharp knife. Sear the scallops for a few seconds on each side until they look tawny brown and caramelised around the edges. Remove from the pan and place on top of the prepared salad. Use a clean scallop shell or similar size dish to serve. Pour the warmed dressing over the top and serve immediately.

Fish Kebabs with
Marmalade Marinade

For 4 bamboo or metal skewers measuring 30cm in
length. Add or subtract ingredients according to choice
of fish and number of people eating with you. Allow 1
skewer per person. Any combination of fish can be used.
Salmon could be used instead of scallops, for example.

For the marinade
1 large red chilli, quartered lengthwise, seeds and white membrane
    removed
2 fat cloves of garlic, crushed
1 piece of root ginger approximately the size of the top of your thumb,
    peeled and grated finely
1 large lemon, zest and juice
1 tbsp Seville orange marmalade
2 cardamom pods, cracked
1 tsp dried coriander seeds, crushed
1 tbsp finely chopped fresh coriander leaves (add the remainder of the
    bunch to the salads)
175ml (6fl oz) olive oil

Whisk together all ingredients in a bowl or jug. Cover
and set aside as you prepare the fish, allowing the flavours
time to blend together.

For the kebabs

large monkfish tail fillet, or 8 monkfish cheeks

8 dived king scallops with orange roe (coral) intact

4 large Scottish langoustine tails, pre-cooked for 1 minute in boiling
     water

2 rashers of streaky bacon

1 medium/large courgette

3 assorted whole peppers in different colours

Ensure that all the grey-coloured membrane is removed from the monkfish tail fillet, as this discolours and goes tough when cooked. Alternatively, if you have obtained monkfish cheeks (which are less expensive) from a fishmonger, check them over and tidy them up. Rinse the scallops under cold water. Remove any trace of the hard ligament if still attached to the side of the cream-coloured flesh. Check and remove any residual 'muck' exuding from the end of the orange coral. Prick the coral once with the point of a sharp knife, but do not remove it. Set aside the whole scallop on dry kitchen paper. (If using salmon instead, remove the skin and cut the fillet into bite-size pieces approximately the same size as the monkfish.) Shell the cooked langoustine tails. Cut each rasher of bacon in half and stretch it with a palette knife on a chopping board to make it thinner. Wrap the stretched bacon around each langoustine in a single layer. This helps protect the langoustine from over-cooking, but gives the bacon a chance to cook thoroughly. Cut the courgette into 8 rounds, approximately 2cm thick. Add any leftover courgette to an accompanying rice or pasta salad, plus perhaps another whole one, both chopped into small pieces. Cut a slice or two from each pepper, avoiding any seeds and white membrane. Cut these slices into pieces, approximately 3cm x 3cm. You will need a total of 16 pieces. The remaining peppers can be chopped small and added to the salad. Put together the kebabs on the skewers. Start with one piece of pepper, skin-side facing your hand. Add one piece of monkfish, followed by one slice of courgette, one whole scallop, one piece of pepper, one prawn, one piece of pepper, scallop, courgette, monkfish, and finish with a piece of pepper, skin facing the end of the skewer. Repeat for all the skewers. Place the kebabs onto a flat baking dish large enough to contain them end-to-end (a lasagne dish, or roasting tin, for example). Pour the marinade over the kebabs. Cover and leave refrigerated for up to 1 hour, until ready to cook, occasionally basting the fish and turning the kebabs over in the marinade. Lift the kebabs from the marinade and grill immediately over a high heat for a few minutes on each side until the fish is cooked and vegetables are charred. The leftover marinade can be warmed gently and a small amount spooned over the cooked kebab, as a dressing, when served.